Live Off Dividends

Achieving Financial Freedom:
The Dividend Investor's Blueprint

Artenie Alexandru

ISBN: 9798377134244

Table of Contents

Foreword

Why am I writing this book? Isn't there already enough information everywhere?

Well, yes, but the amount of information is simply overwhelming. From Books and Blogs to YouTube Channels and Paid Courses, it takes work for a beginner investor to find and filter all the information he needs.

Here my mission starts. This book aims to collect and filter the best of my experience as a retail investor and present it to beginner investors simply and understandably. My target is that after reading this book, you get the basic knowledge and techniques to make you steps through your investing journey confidently.

Disclaimer

Nothing presented in this book shall be treated as investment advice.

All the content and stock analysis shall be considered for informational purposes only.

Make sure you research before investing your money and understand that your capital is at risk.

1. General Advice for Investing in Dividend Stocks

There are some good things to know, and it is generally valid for investing and it's good to keep in mind if you want to be a successful investor.

Be a long-term Investor

Regarding dividend investing, it's generally better to adopt a long-term investment strategy rather than a short-term trading approach. Being a long-term investor is essentially a matter of mindset and behavior. For example, it may be easy to purchase a stock, but when the stock's value drops and you find yourself with a 30% loss, it can be challenging to have faith in its future recovery and avoid selling.

Sometimes, stocks in your portfolio go down by as much as 35%. This can be disappointing, but it also means you can buy those same stocks at a lower price. This is called buying at a discount, meaning you can get the stock for less money and benefit from its future growth.

In summary, if some of your stocks are currently down, do not sell them. Instead, keep them for the long term, for at least 5-10 years, and see how they perform over time. This approach is known as a buy-and-hold strategy. It aims to maximize returns by holding onto an asset for an extended period, regardless of short-term market fluctuations.

To say it differently, don't sell a stock based on the current price compared to the price at the purchase. Instead, sell only if you are no longer confident in the business of that particular company.

Choose Your Investing Strategy

Before investing, make a plan that suits your goals and risk tolerance. For example, decide if you want to focus on growth, dividends, or a balance of both. Then, please write it down and stick to it, no matter what happens in the market.

If you are now 30 years old and don't need the money from your stocks, you can re-invest everything and add extra monthly cash to your portfolio.

The amount which you add every month or quarter is up to you. Still, I highly recommend adding money from your salary until your portfolio is big enough to generate much more than you can add every month/quarter.

Dividend re-investing is necessary because your portfolio will significantly outgrow others who did not re-invest the dividends later.

When building a portfolio, it is possible to include a mix of different types of stocks, such as those with a small yield but high growth potential, those with a balance of yield and growth, and others that pay a high dividend yield but may not experience significant stock price growth, such as utility stocks.

So, decide at least these things before you go any further.

Select Your Brokerage Account

Why do you need a brokerage account? These firms are the connections between us investors and the stock exchange. Only through them is it possible to buy ETFs, Stocks, and so on.

Many firms are offering this type of service, also your local bank probably (but it will most likely be the most expensive choice). So, Google for a spreadsheet or a good comparison between firms available in your country.

As a dividend investor, be looking for these facts:

- **Monthly fee?** The best is where you don't have to pay a monthly fee; there are some companies.

- **Inactivity fee?** Also, look for companies where you don't have to pay an inactivity fee. For example, if you don't have the money to pay in and invest, the company won't charge you any for the inactivity.

- **Dividend fee?** When you receive your portion of a dividend from a company, your brokerage won't charge you because they add this amount to your account.

- Look for the **lowest transaction** fee when you buy a stock.

- **Money withdrawal**. When withdrawing some money from your account, it „has to be" free. And mostly, it is.

- **Money Protection/Investor protection**. If your broker goes bankrupt, you must know how much money will be returned to you. Some brokerage accounts offer more protection than others, starting from $20,000 up to $100,000-$300,000 or even more. I suggest starting with a brokerage that provides at least

$20,000 in protection, and later on, when your portfolio grows, you can consider switching to one that offers more protection.

If you go through these points after that, you will have a pretty good picture of which brokerage company to choose.

2. Dividend Lingo

Understanding dividend-related terminology can be the key to unlocking higher investment returns.

By learning about terms such as dividend yield, payout ratio, and ex-dividend date, you can identify companies with a history of paying consistent and reliable dividends. This can help you build a portfolio of stocks that not only have the potential for capital appreciation but also provide a steady income stream.

Additionally, by understanding the tax implications of dividends, you can make strategic decisions that can help boost your overall returns. In short, taking the time to understand dividend-related terminology is an investment in your financial future.

So, let's get started!

What is a Dividend in Stocks

A dividend is a payment a company makes to its shareholders. It's a portion of the company's earnings, decided by the board of directors, given to shareholders. Dividends can be given in cash, shares of stock, or other forms.

When a company makes a profit, it can either keep the money or give some of it to shareholders as dividends. The dividend is usually a fixed amount or stock price percentage.

Dividend-paying stocks can be a good investment choice for those who want a steady income, but it's important to remember that dividends aren't guaranteed and can change or stop.

You can easily find the dividend paid by a particular company using different tools, usually for free. Here is how you can see it for AAPL on a simple "Dividend AAPL" Google Search:

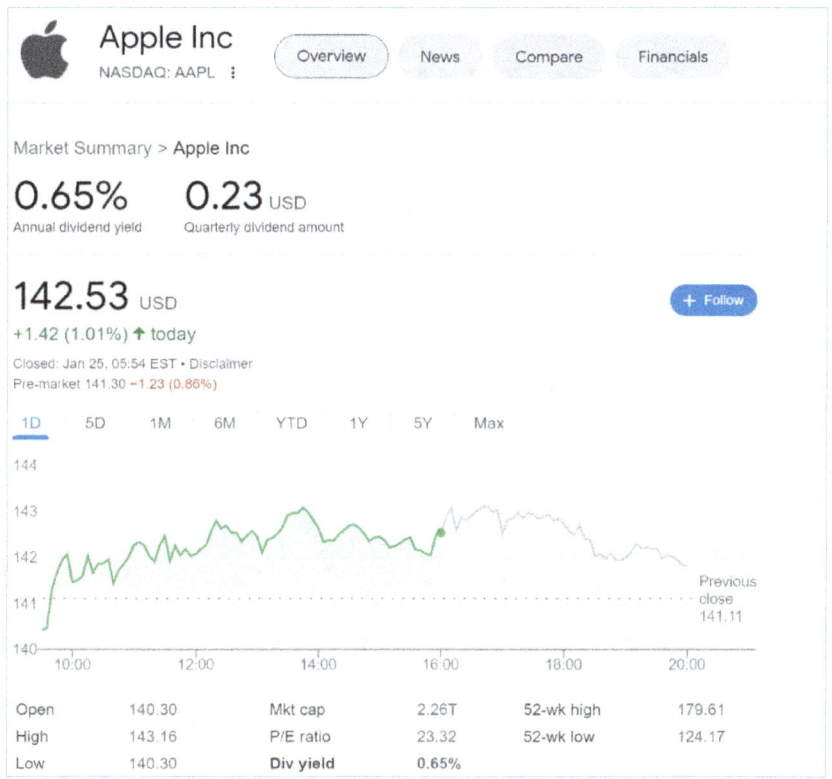

Figure 1 - Dividend of Apple. Source: Google Search

What is Dividend Tax Rates

Dividend tax rates refer to the tax that investors have to pay on the dividends they receive from owning shares in a company. The dividend tax rate can vary depending on the country or jurisdiction where the investor resides and the type of dividends received.

In some countries, the dividend tax rate can be lower than the tax rate on other types of income, such as interest or capital gains, to encourage investment in companies.

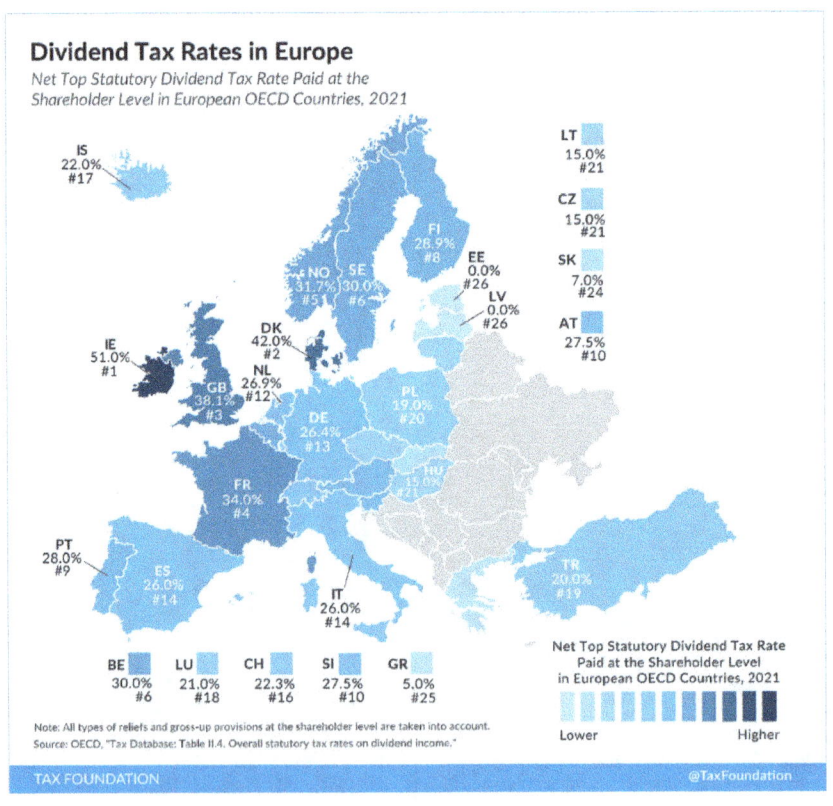

Figure 2- Dividend Tax Rates in Europe. Source: www.taxfoundation.org

You can find the dividend tax rate for your country using www.OECD.stat.

Although it is an essential subject, dividend taxation is a tricky matter. They depend from state to state and individual to individual. This is why I don't give more information here so that I do not create confusion.

It's important to note that the tax laws are subject to change and are different by country; it's always a good idea to check with a professional tax advisor or your local tax office to understand the tax rules and regulations that apply to you.

Calculating the Dividend Yield

The dividend yield is a way to measure how much money you will get back from a stock investment based on the dividends paid by the company. It is usually shown as a percentage of the current stock price. To calculate it, you divide the annual dividends by the stock price:

Dividend Yield = (Annual Dividend per Share) /

(Current Stock Price per Share)

For example, if a stock is $50 and pays $1.50 in dividends per year, the dividend yield is 3% (1.5 / 50 = 0.03).

Although you usually don't have to calculate it by yourself, as it is publicly given, it is helpful to understand how those numbers are calculated.

Below is a real example using the dividend of AT&T Inc. (T):

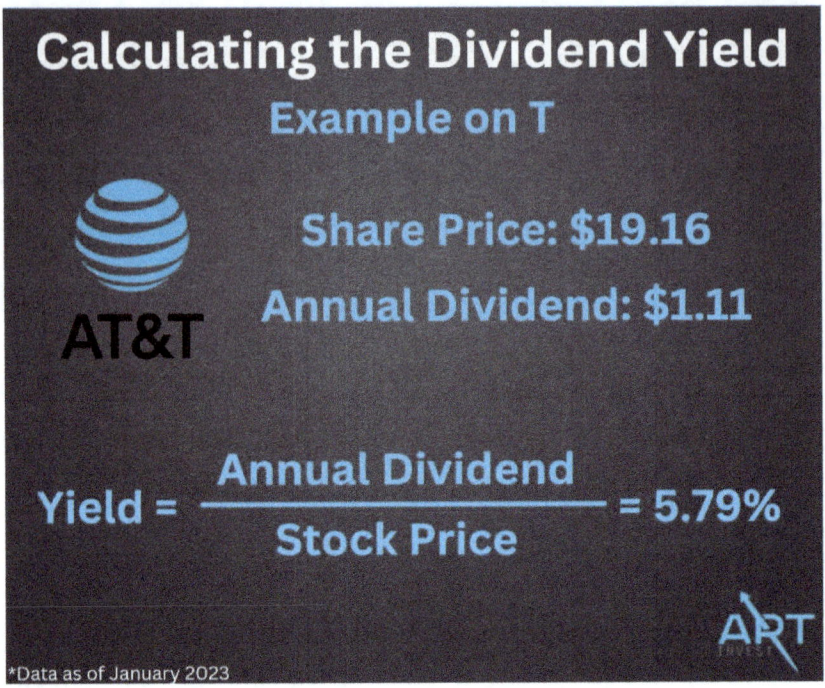

Figure 3 - Calculating the Dividend Yield. Example on AT&T stock.

It's important to remember that dividend yield does not guarantee future performance, and companies can change or stop dividends. Also, stock price changes can affect the dividend yield. So it's a good idea to research the company and its financial health before investing.

What is the Dividend Payout Ratio

The dividend payout ratio is a way to measure how much of a company's profits are given to shareholders as dividends. It's shown as a percentage, which you calculate by dividing the dividends paid per share by the earnings per share (EPS).

Payout Ratio = (Annual Dividend per Share) /

(Earnings per Share)

For example, if a company has an EPS of $2 and pays $1 in dividends, the payout ratio is 50% (1/$2).

Below is a real example using Dividend for Altria Group Inc (MO):

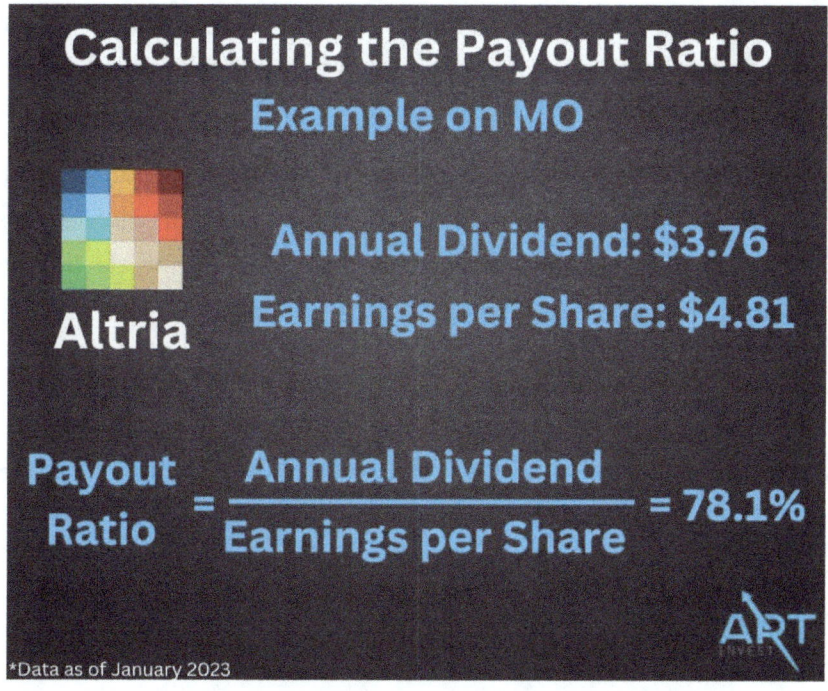

Figure 4 - Calculating the Payout Ratio. Example of Dividend for MO

A low payout ratio means the company is keeping more of its profits to invest or pay the debt, while a high payout ratio means the company is giving more profits to shareholders.

It's important to remember that a high payout ratio can also mean the company may not have enough profits to pay future dividends or invest.

What are Ex-Dividend Dates

The ex-dividend date is when a stock is traded without the right to its most recently declared dividend. If you buy a stock on or after the ex-dividend date, you won't be able to receive the next dividend payment. This means the stock is traded "ex-dividend" (without the dividend).

It's important to remember that the ex-dividend date is not the same as the payment date, which is when the dividend is paid to the shareholders. Investors should keep in mind the ex-dividend date when buying or selling stocks to make sure they receive dividends or not.

To ensure you are eligible to receive the dividends, buy the stock before the ex-dividend date and hold it until after the record date.

What is a Dividend Record Date

The record date is when a company makes a list of its shareholders to decide who will receive the dividends. The company will check its list of shareholders on this date, and whoever is on the list will receive the dividends. It is usually set one day after the ex-dividend date.

The company will usually close its books on the record date, which means you will only get the upcoming dividends if you buy the stock after this date. However, investors should pay attention to the record date to make sure they will receive the dividends if they own the stock on this date. The record date is usually set after the ex-dividend date and before the payment date.

When is the Dividend Paid

The dividend payment date, also known as the "payment date," is the date on which the company distributes the dividends to its shareholders. This date is set by the company's board of directors and is usually announced along with the dividend amount and ex-dividend date.

On the payment date, the dividends are paid out to shareholders who were on the company's books on the record date. Therefore, investors need to pay attention to the payment date to ensure they receive their dividends and plan for the cash flow. The payment date is usually set after the ex-dividend date and the record date.

How Often is a Dividend Paid

Dividends are typically paid regularly, such as quarterly or annually. Some companies pay dividends monthly or semi-annually, but this is rare. The frequency at which a company pays dividends is determined by its board of directors and is typically based on its financial performance and cash flow.

21

Quarterly dividends are paid four times a year, typically at the end of each quarter. As a result, companies that pay quarterly dividends tend to have a stable financial performance and cash flow and pay consistent dividends over time.

You can easily find What Ex-Dividend Dates are, What is the Dividend Record Date, When is the Dividend Paid, and When is the Dividend Paid for a particular stock using publicly available information. Here is how this information looks on SeekingAlpha in the case of Dividends for IBM:

Figure 5 - Dividend for IBM. Source: www.seekingalpha.com

Investing in a REIT

REITs own and operate income-producing real estates, such as buildings and properties. They allow individual investors to invest in these real estate portfolios, similar to how they might invest in other industries through stocks.

REITs pay out a large portion of their income as dividends to shareholders, making them a good source of steady income. They can be publicly traded on stock exchanges or privately held and can focus on specific types of properties or be diversified.

REITs offer a way for people to invest in real estate without owning and managing properties themselves. However, keep in mind that REITs have the same risks as other publicly traded companies and can be affected by changes in the real estate market.

Some of the most reliable REITs, according to Forbes, are:

1. Stag Industrial (STAG)

2. Realty Income (O)

3. Omega Healthcare Investors (OHI)

4. Medical Properties (MPW)

5. Iron Mountain (IRM)

6. Crown Castle (CCI)

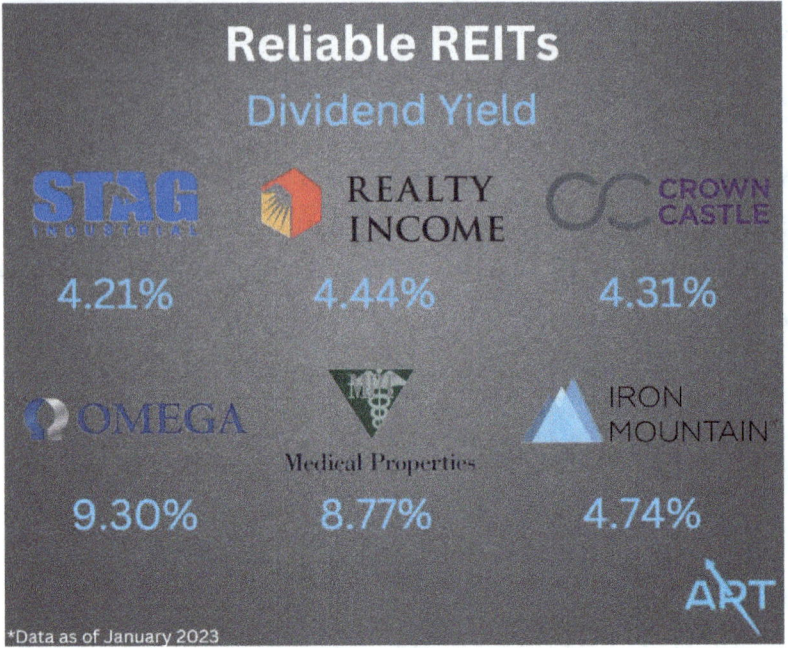

Figure 6 – Some REITs Dividends

Blue Chip Stocks with Dividends

Blue chip stocks are shares of well-established and financially stable companies with a long history of consistent growth and a strong track record of paying dividends. These companies are typically leaders in their industry and have a reputation for providing a stable return on investment.

Blue chip stocks are considered less risky than other types of stocks, as they are less likely to be affected by market fluctuations or economic downturns.

The Dow Jones Industrial Average (DJIA) is an index that comprises 30 blue-chip stocks that are considered to be the leaders in their respective industries.

Some examples of blue-chip stocks are:

24

1. General Electric (GE)

2. Procter & Gamble (PG)

3. Coca-Cola (KO)

4. Home Depot Inc. (HD)

5. Walmart (WMT)

6. Visa (V)

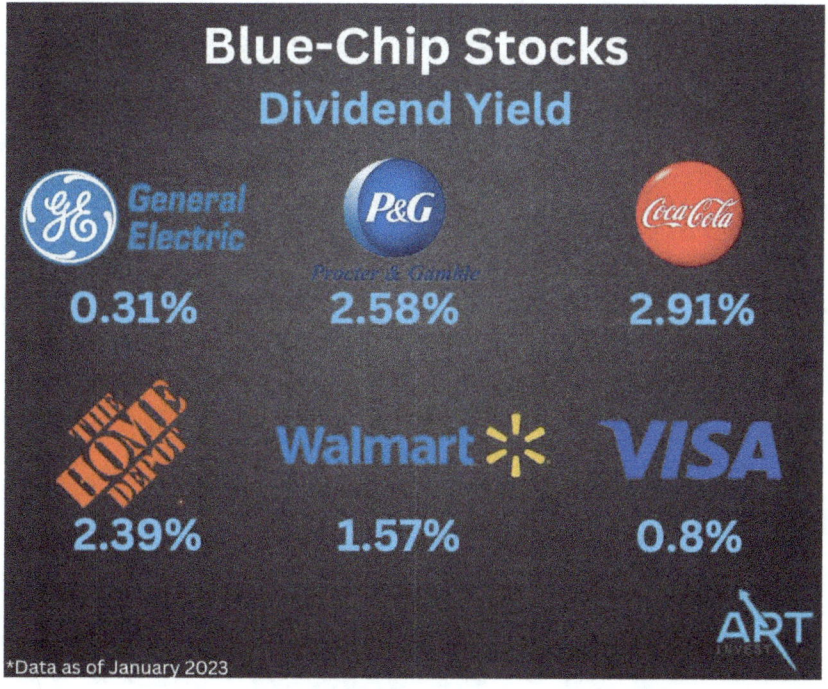

Figure 7 - Blue Chip Stocks with Dividends

It's important to note that while blue chip stocks are generally considered less risky, they are still subject to market fluctuations and the specific company's performance. Therefore, it's essential to do your research and consult with a financial advisor before making any investment decisions.

Bottom Line

In summary, understanding dividend terminology is crucial for making informed investment decisions and evaluating the performance of a company's stock. Familiarizing oneself with terms such as dividend yield, payout ratio, and ex-dividend date can help investors make more strategic decisions and increase their returns.

3. How to pick a dividend stock

Okay, so you have the mindset, your brokerage account, and you learned the basic terms.

Let's start, but where?

You should read articles, guides, and books like this and watch videos for at least 2-3 months before investing. If you do so, you will repeatedly hear names, which you can look into and research using the methods presented in this book.

But if you don't know where to start, here is your crutch: Download this „Dividend Radar" list. It will be updated every month, and it contains everything that we need!

In there, you will find a list of the dividend champions. They have a dividend-paying and increasing record of 25+ years. Contenders have a 10+ years record. Challengers are a bit risky with only 5-9 years of history.

This list, as I said, can be beneficial and contains many pieces of information; it will continuously be updated monthly!

Which are the best dividend paying stocks?

First of all, don't go only for the big dividend yields. You can easily make this mistake if you want to jump into this world as quickly as possible. You will lose money if you are targeting only the companies paying the biggest yields!

If you see a stock that offers a yield above 10%, then better run. It is mostly a trap; the yield will be cut soon, and the stock price will be very volatile. Not a good idea to invest in it.

So, as I suggest: a **minimum of 10 years** of dividend record. It is important because, in this way, we can estimate that the company will continue to pay and raise its dividends. Of course, there are other metrics also to look at, but overall, this is a good starting point, and you have a list with more than 350 stocks with many pieces of information. Much better than going through the hundreds of thousands of available stocks.

Many dividend-paying stocks can be considered "best," depending on your investment goals and risk tolerance.

What is Good Dividend Yield

A good dividend yield can vary depending on the industry. A typical yield for S&P500 companies is between 1-2%. Some blue-chip companies, such as utility companies or telecom companies, have a yield of around 4-5%.

Below is a chart showing Dividend Yields by Sector for Large Cap U.S. Companies as of June 2022, according to https://siblisresearch.com/.

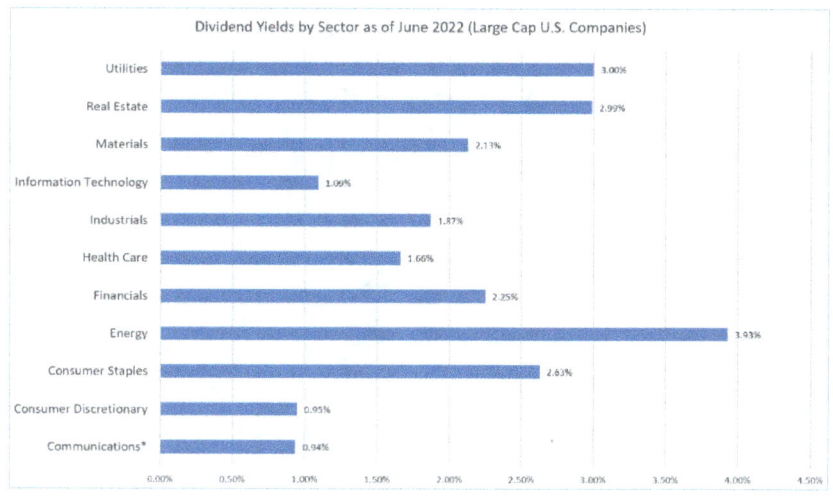

Figure 8 - Dividend Yields by Sector for Large Cap U.S. Companies as of June 2022

Any yield above the average for a particular sector is a good deal.

Stocks with Dividend Growth

Many stocks have a history of increasing their dividends over time, known as dividend growth. Some examples of stocks with a long-term record of dividend growth include:

Johnson & Johnson (**JNJ**) – 6.03% (5-year growth rate, per annum) for 60 years

Procter & Gamble (**PG**) – 5.68%, for 66 years

Coca-Cola (**KO**) – 3.53%, for 60 years

PepsiCo (**PEP**) – 7.39%, for 50 years

3M (**MMM**) – 4.86%, 64 years

T. Rowe Price Group (**TROW**) – 16.05%, for 36 years

Lockheed Martin (**LMT**) – 8.85%, for 20 years

McDonald's (**MCD**) – 8.12%, for 21 years

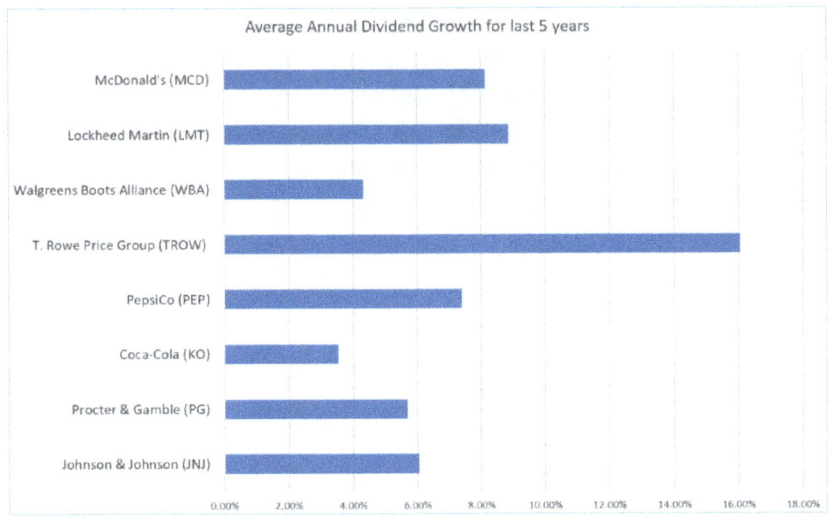

Figure 9 – Average Annual Dividend Growth Rate for the last five years of some well-established companies

Although not presented here, there are many companies with above 10% of annual dividend growth. However, they usually have a short dividend payment history.

It's important to note that future dividends and dividend growth rates are not guaranteed, and that past performance does not indicate future results. Therefore, before investing in any stock, it's crucial to conduct research and consider your investment objectives and risk tolerance.

Best Dividend Stocks for Long Term

I bet you got the idea so far. Although past performance is not a guarantee of future results, it might be good to have a solid base composed of established dividend payers combined with a few new and promising companies to spice up your portfolio.

We will analyze a potential portfolio in Chapter 7 of this book.

After your First Some Stocks

Many famous investors agree with the rule of 25. If you have more than 25 stocks in your portfolio, you are more likely to not understand every business you have in your portfolio; you can't track and follow every news about them and make decisions. More than 25 stocks aren't helping anymore with the diversification either.

I suggest the following: begin with the amount you want. If it is something small, invest in only one company, and after that, add another company into your portfolio and slowly build it until you reach the 10th stock. Then make sure that you have in each stock 1000$ and then go for the 11th, 12th, and so on.

How much do you need to Invest to Live Off Dividends

You will need a lot of money to live off the dividends and somehow retire or do whatever you want with your time.

How much is it? This is a complex question.

Let's say that you need $1000 for your monthly expenses. That is $12,000 per year. We will use this round number as an example so that you can easily scale up to your needs.

The dividend yield is important to discuss in the first place. Live off is like a retirement plan, so you will need stocks or ETFs with a higher dividend yield, little or decent growth in dividends, and not-so-volatile stock prices.

An Apple stock can be a good investment but is not suggested in a retirement portfolio because it pays out currently only a 0.51% dividend yield. This isn't good to live off the dividends because you will need a lot of money to get to the 1000$ monthly.

On the other side, watch out for very high yields, as already mentioned.

It is optimal to have a balanced portfolio with a mix of different investments. For example, consider investing in a company like Starbucks (SBUX), which has strong growth potential but only pays a small dividend, and also investing in a company like Enterprise Products Partners (EPD), which pays a high dividend but has limited growth potential.

Additionally, it's also a good idea to invest in companies with moderate dividends and good growth potential.

Let's be slightly pessimistic and say that after taxes, the whole portfolio has to have a payout ratio of 3.5%. And I will present as an example the worst-case scenario of taxation, which is 30%.

You will see the gross dividend yield on the research sites, so before tax, you will need a 5% average yield from your portfolio. From here, we can calculate that the 12000$ net dividend becomes with the 30% tax = $17,142.

For this amount and the 5% gross yield, you will have to invest $342,840!

What to do next?

Let's say you have the money but aren't an expert; then talk to an expert about investing this much money. Not to a guy who sells life insurance and so an...a real somebody who is an expert about dividend investing.

Over time, your income from dividends will grow larger than just receiving a fixed $1000 per month. This is because some companies may increase their dividends by only a small percentage each year, while others may increase them by a much larger percentage. As a result, your portfolio will provide you with an annual "pay raise" that is not directly tied to the share price of the companies but will result in you earning more money in total.

This is nice and everything, but what if you don't have the money yet for it but don't have 30 years to retire?

Well, the more time you have, the less amount you have to begin with, and if you have less time but want to start with a larger amount or put a larger amount into the portfolio every month, it may be enough. And don't forget about dividend re-investment since it works similarly to compounding interest.

Dividend Reinvesting

If you're an investor looking to build wealth over the long term, dividend reinvesting might be the tool you need to help you reach your financial goals.

By reinvesting your dividends, you can increase your overall holdings in the investment and experience compounding growth over time. In this section, we'll explore the benefits of dividend reinvesting and why it's a powerful tool for long-term investors.

What is Dividend Reinvesting?

Dividend reinvesting is a way to automatically reinvest the dividends you earn from your investments into the same asset. When you receive dividends, instead of receiving cash, the dividends are used to purchase additional shares or units in the investment. Over time, this can help you accumulate more shares and potentially lead to greater returns.

It is many times referred to as DRIP (Dividend Re-Investment Plan).

Benefits of Dividend Reinvesting

Compounded Growth: One of the most significant benefits of dividend reinvesting is the potential for compounded growth. By reinvesting your dividends, you can increase your overall holdings in the investment and experience compounded growth over time. This means your returns could be higher in the long term than receiving the dividends as cash.

Dollar-Cost Averaging: Another benefit of dividend reinvesting is that it allows you to take advantage of dollar-cost averaging. Dollar-cost averaging is an investment strategy where you invest a fixed amount of money into an investment at regular intervals. By reinvesting your dividends, you are making additional investments into the same stock, which can help average the cost per share over time.

Convenient and Automated: Dividend reinvesting is a convenient and automated process. Once you set up dividend reinvesting, you don't have to worry about manually reinvesting your dividends. Instead, the process happens automatically, saving you time and effort.

Drawbacks of Dividend Reinvesting

Taxes: One of the drawbacks of dividend reinvesting is that you may have to pay taxes on the dividends you receive. Your taxes will depend on your country's tax laws and your tax situation.

Investment Expenses: Another drawback of dividend reinvesting is that you may have to pay investment expenses, such as management fees or transaction costs. These expenses can reduce your returns over time, so it's essential to consider them when deciding whether to reinvest dividends or receive them as cash.

Let's do an experiment.

It is straightforward. We have to imagine two cases:

1. Invest in O (Realty Income Corporation) back in 1994 and **harvest the dividends.**
2. Invest in O back in 1994 and **re-invest the dividends.**

Then we have to back-test these two portfolios using PortfolioVisualizer.

Here is how portfolio 1 would have performed till January 2023:

Figure 10 – Portfolio 1 performance (no dividend re-investment)

The above picture shows that your $10,000 initial investment would turn in these 19 years into $84,211, plus $59,905 in dividends, meaning you earned $134,116.

Remember this number, and let's move to Portfolio 2.

Here is the performance of the same investment and period, but re-investing the dividends instead pulling the money out.

Figure 11 - Portfolio 2 performance (with dividend re-invested)

I have triple-checked the results. The numbers speak for themselves. While investing the same amount of money for the same period, Portfolio 2 with re-invested dividends tremendously outperformed Portfolio 1 with no re-investment.

The reason is simple. The extra shares bought using dividends generated additional returns and extra dividends, which produced new returns and new dividends, which in turn ... you got the point. This is the power of compounding.

"Compound interest is the eighth wonder of the world."

- Albert Einstein

The compounding effect applies to stock returns, interest rates, or dividends.

We got a simple compounding interest calculator on our website, encouraging you to experiment with and plan your financial future. Here is an example showing what it looks like:

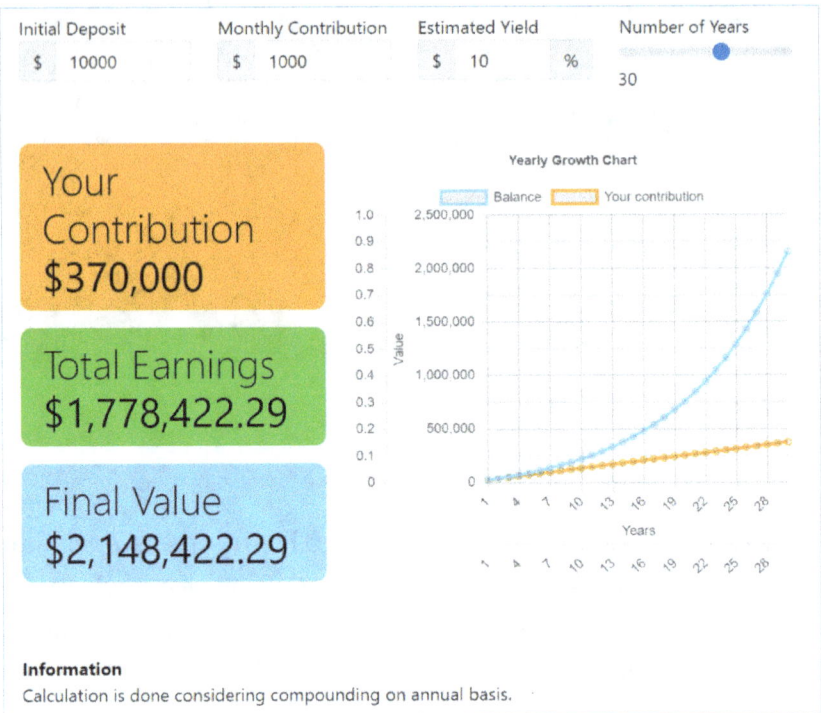

Figure 12 – Compounding Interest Calculator Example. Source: www.art-invest.net

Adding Dividends Growth

Since we dived into numbers in this section, let's do an additional math exercise and combine the concepts of dividend re-investing and dividend growth.

Just for the example's sake, let's pick an imaginary stock, with a price of $100 per share with an annual return of 7% and a dividend yield of 5%, that we will re-invest (we learned the lesson above).

Now, we want to evaluate dividend growth's impact on portfolio performance. For this evaluation, I will use the Dividend Calculator from TIPRANKS.

38

Here is the setup:

Figure 13 – Dividend Calculator. No Dividend Increase

So, you invested $10,000 and bought 100 shares. In 20 years, you end up with a portfolio end balance of $98,104.

Nothing unexpected so far. Now, let's rerun the calculator, but we will assume a 10% annual dividend yield increase this time.

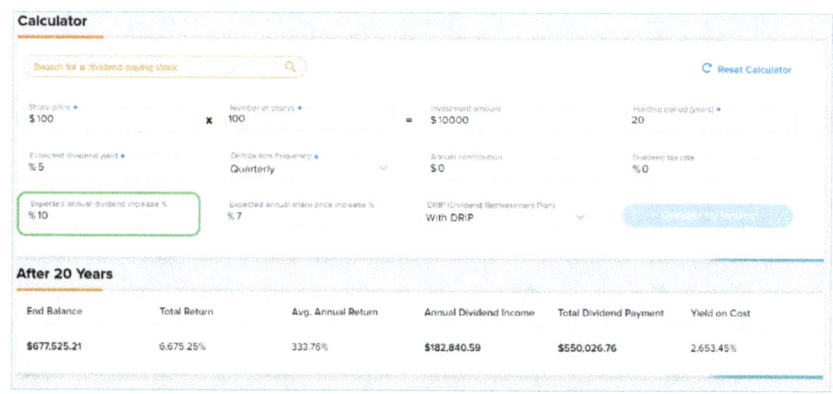

Figure 14 - Dividend Calculator. 10% Annual Dividend Increase

As you can see, the results of the imaginary stock led to similar conclusions as the results of Realty Income stock, even if the annual dividend growth in its case is significantly lower (the imaginary 10% was an incredibly optimistic figure).

End words

I am sure you learned some important principles here. With time, you will master and apply them successfully. However, what is most important is to BEGIN! Begin to invest as soon as possible to generate wealth for yourself and your family. Of course, you are lucky if you have the money to live off 1000$ of monthly dividends, but if you don't, don't be sad. You will get there, I'm sure!

4. Dividend Stock Analysis Example

Before we start, please note that the following analysis is for educational purposes. The figures presented below might need to be updated, depending on when you purchased the book; however, the methodology is valid at any time. The data used in the following analysis is as of the end of January 2023.

Let's pick Cummins (CMI)

Cummins Inc. designs, manufactures, distributes, and services diesel and natural gas engines, electric and hybrid powertrains, and related components worldwide. It operates through five segments: Engine, Distribution, Components, Power Systems, and New Power.

The company offers diesel and natural gas-powered engines under the Cummins and other customer brands for the heavy and medium-duty truck, bus, recreational vehicle, light-duty automotive, construction, mining, marine, rail, oil and gas, defense, and agricultural markets; and offers new parts and services, as well as remanufactured parts and engines.

So, first criteria: Cummins has a dividend record of 17 years of dividend-paying and increasing. Thus, this is a healthy check mark.

Let's reform the list from DividendRadar. You can hide some columns to begin and get a better overview. For example, hide FV from „Current DIV" to „52-week range – high" in all eight columns. This information isn't that important when investing for the long term.

You will have a picture something like this:

January 27, 2023							Dividend Growth				
Symbol	Company	Sector	No Years	Price	Div Yield	5Y Avg Yield	DGR 1Y	DGR 3Y	DGR 5Y	DGR 10Y	Fair Value
CMI	Cummins Inc.	Industrials	17	247.78	2.53	2.70	7.86	7.21	7.49	12.87	At Fair Value

Figure 15 – CMI Stock as presented in the list from DividendRadar

Here I have to make a quick note about Diversification if it is your first stock.

There are many quotes, but I want to express only the ones from Warren Buffett.

- *„Don't put every egg of yours into one basket!"* ☐

- *„Never test the depth of the river with both feet!"* ☐

In other words, if you put all of your money into one stock, then if it fails, you lose your money also. If it fails dramatically, then you may not be able to handle all the stress, and you sell every position and lose money.

Of course, there is always a slight percent chance that this one stock will go high in the first year, and if you sell, you will end up with a good amount of extra money, but it is mostly just speculation, and I don't like to speculate.

As you can see from this example, it isn't safe to play like this. That's why it is vital to buy stocks in different sectors. In this way, your portfolio will be well diversified. Sometimes one will rise, and others will soar. This is how the world functions; diversifying wisely is the only way to go against it.

More about that is in Chapter 7.

Real Research

Let's begin with what we can read out from this Excel Spreadsheet.

- How many years do they pay and increase their dividends? – **17years**

- The price isn't a piece of good information because it changes every day, so **ignore that**.

- The dividend yield is correct but **changes** with the current stock price.

- The 5-year average yield is a good indicator to see if the current dividend yield is much greater or worse than this.

- DGR numbers? What are they? This is the percentage by how much they have increased their dividends recently, 3-year average, 5-year average, and 10-year average. Here you have to look for TWO things. First, the amount by how much they increased has to be around the same over the years. As you can see, it is about the same or more, so **this is a checkmark for me**. Secondly, the current increase (DGR1y) plus the current dividend yield is greater than 9%? **Definitely yes!**

- Fair value column: If there is either „At fair value" or „In the margin of safety," you are good to go! You don't want to see here the text „Overvalued."

After the Spreadsheet…

This was all the important information that could be given to us in this Spreadsheet. Let's open one of the most used research sites to look deeper into the stock:

Yahoo! Finance

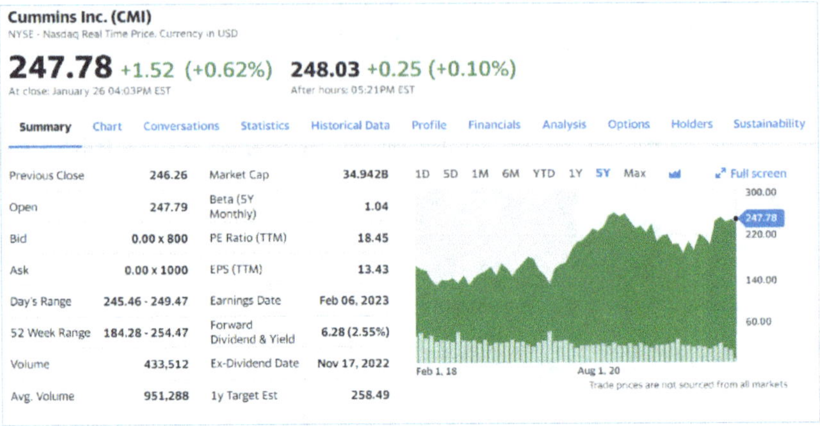

Figure 16 – CMI Stock as presented by Yahoo! Finance

- Next step is to take a look at the **P/E ratio**. As one of the greatest investors wrote in his book, this ratio must be under 25. In CMI's case, it is only 18.45.

- Next one is a little bit difficult, **Share buybacks**. Share buybacks can be a silent killer for your investment. If a company is issuing shares repeatedly, your slice of the cake will be diluted. So, we are looking for share buybacks, not the other way around. Go to the „Financials" tab on Yahoo! Finance and look for these rows:

| Summary | Chart | Conversations | Statistics | Historical Data | Profile | **Financials** | Analysis |

Show: **Income Statement**   Balance Sheet   Cash Flow

Income Statement   All numbers in thousands

Breakdown	TTM	12/30/2021	12/30/2020	12/30/2019
> Total Revenue	26,154,000	24,021,000	19,811,000	23,571,000
Cost of Revenue	19,937,000	18,326,000	14,917,000	17,591,000
Gross Profit	6,217,000	5,695,000	4,894,000	5,980,000
> Operating Expense	3,915,000	3,481,000	3,047,000	3,467,000
Operating Income	2,302,000	2,214,000	1,847,000	2,513,000
> Net Non Operating Interest Inc...	-102,000	-86,000	-96,000	-74,000
> Other Income Expense	354,000	623,000	587,000	395,000
Pretax Income	2,555,000	2,751,000	2,338,000	2,834,000
Tax Provision	616,000	587,000	527,000	566,000
> Net Income Common Stockhold...	1,914,000	2,131,000	1,789,000	2,260,000
Diluted NI Available to Com Stock...	1,914,000	2,131,000	1,789,000	2,260,000
Basic EPS	-	14.74	12.07	14.54
Diluted EPS	-	14.61	12.01	14.48
Basic Average Shares	-	144,600	148,200	155,400
Diluted Average Shares	-	145,900	149,000	156,100

Figure 17 – Income Statement of CMI as presented on Yahoo! Finance

The first column is from 2021, the second from 2020, and so on… as you can see, the number of outstanding shares has been declining over the years, so CMI also does an excellent job and diligently buys back shares every year. (All numbers are in thousands.)

- In the end, let's look at the dividend yield. Right now, it is 2.55%, which is a decent yield! CMI is considered a more growth stock than a dividend payer; this fact can be seen in the 5-year average yield. Around 2.70% average yield is excellent for a growth stock and reasonable for a dividend stock; that's why it is a great opportunity to buy into CMI.

Let's talk about the increase for a little

This isn't a big deal if you don't want to dig into this world deeper, but it can also be helpful.

One rule which you have to hold in your mind every time. „Dividends aren't mandatory payments!" The company decides if they want to pay some and how much actually...

That's why our best interest is to find out if they are willing to pay. A perfect metric to find this out is to look at the dividend increase year by year. As I mentioned earlier, these numbers are in the Excel Spreadsheet marked „DGR" numbers - Dividend Growth Rate.

Dividend Safety/Coverage

Yes, it is good when the company has a dividend record and other things, but it doesn't make sense if your dividend is paid from newly issued debt or newly issued shares, for example.

You might find out this information, but to understand it better, you must do some calculations. The best place to start can be Yahoo Finance which I'm using too. After you search your stock, go to the „Financials" – „Cash Flow" – Click „Expand all" and here we are.

| Summary | Chart | Conversations | Statistics | Historical Data | Profile | Financials | Analysis |

Show: Income Statement   Balance Sheet   **Cash Flow**

Cash Flow   All numbers in thousands

Breakdown	TTM	12/30/2021	12/30/2020	12/30/2019
> Operating Cash Flow	1,877,000	2,256,000	2,722,000	3,181,000
> Investing Cash Flow	-4,091,000	-873,000	-719,000	-1,150,000
⌄ Financing Cash Flow	1,963,000	-2,227,000	280,000	-2,095,000
⌄ Cash Flow from Continuing Fi...	1,963,000	-2,227,000	280,000	-2,095,000
> Net Issuance Payments of ...	3,313,000	-32,000	1,614,000	-163,000
> Net Common Stock Issuan...	-479,000	-1,346,000	-553,000	-1,271,000
> Cash Dividends Paid	-841,000	-809,000	-782,000	-761,000
Net Other Financing Charges	-30,000	-40,000	1,000	100,000
> End Cash Position	2,337,000	2,592,000	3,401,000	1,129,000
Capital Expenditure	-885,000	-786,000	-575,000	-775,000
Issuance of Capital Stock	65,000	56,000	88,000	.
Issuance of Debt	2,120,000	79,000	2,024,000	53,000
Repayment of Debt	-1,086,000	-73,000	-410,000	-216,000
Repurchase of Capital Stock	-544,000	-1,402,000	-641,000	-1,271,000
Free Cash Flow	992,000	1,470,000	2,147,000	2,406,000

Figure 18 – Cash Flow Statement of CMI as presented by Yahoo! Finance

Using those two metrics, we will need to calculate the dividend payout ratio! I always compare this to the Free cash flow. Most companies pay their dividends out from the Free Cash Flow. I want to ensure they have enough from that and that the paid dividends aren't higher than the Free Cash Flows by 75%.

If the paid dividends are higher than the Free Cash Flow, the dividend is unsafe and will likely be cut in the next few years. So I can begin to worry because when the company wants to maintain its dividends, it will issue shares for this purpose or go into more debt. (I have already seen something like this.).

Let's use the first column, which is a trailing number.

841,000 / 992,000 = 84.7% the payout ratio

As you can figure out, the current payout ratio could be more attractive. Thus, we should be careful.

Dividend yield at its best?

Unfortunately, there aren't many more metrics we can use for free, but let's go to another site. SeekingAlpha.

Seeking Alpha is similar to Yahoo! Finance or Morningstar.com, but you will find a good piece of information under this link. Scroll down a little bit, and you will see Cummins's Dividend yield percentage history. As you can see, the yield is at its height right now.

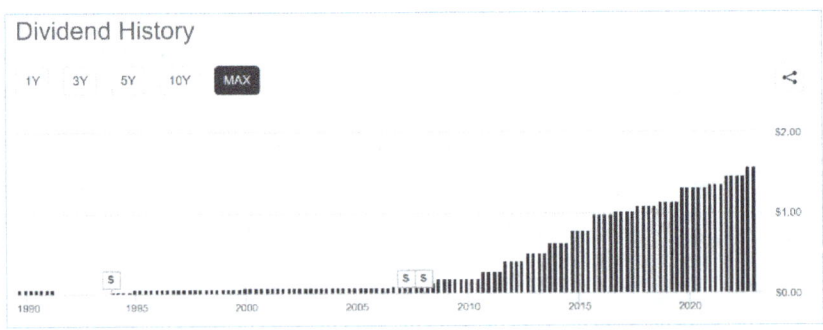

Figure 19 – CMI Dividend History as presented by SeekingAlpha

5. Dividend ETFs

Suppose you are young like me; you probably want to pull out the money later in life. So, you don't need that much of a dividend. Of course, it's good to have and reinvest it, but to be safer, I suggest giving a small portion of your portfolio to an ETF.

An Exchange-Traded Fund, aka ETF

The most famous one is SPY, which tracks the S&P 500 index. There are 500 stocks in this index. So, if, let's say, 50 companies don't perform well, there are another 450 companies in the index that do perform well. Then the index will continue to grow. It is like you diversifying your small amount of investment between 500 companies. You don't have to buy each one of them separately. Just buy the ETF which holds them.

If you are a European citizen, you can't buy US ETFs. I have to copy-paste to explain this:

„ *Unless you prove you're a 'sophisticated investor', practically all platforms and brokers will refuse to sell you ETFs based in the US (also known as US-domiciled or US-registered ETFs) because* **these products do not conform to European UCITS regulation.**"

This is just a short explanation, but the critical part you need to know is there.

49

So where can I buy ETFs? On the German stock exchange mainly. Many ETFs out there copy the S&P500, for example, and many other famous indexes from the US.

One of my favorites is the „**iShares Core MSCI World UCITS ETF USD.**" In this ETF, there are more than 1700 companies from all over the world. An excellent approach to ETFs is to buy them over and over again. It doesn't matter what the price is. Just buy and forget about it.

Dividend in ETF

Dividend-paying ETFs are exchange-traded funds that focus on companies that pay dividends to shareholders. These dividends can provide a steady stream of income for investors and can also serve as a signal of a company's financial health.

Dividend-paying ETFs may be a good choice for investors looking for regular income, but it's important to note that they may not perform as well in a rising-rate environment.

Additionally, dividend-paying ETFs may have a different risk profile than non-dividend-paying ETFs, so it's essential to consider the potential risks and rewards before investing.

Distribution vs. Accumulation Dividend ETFs

Distribution and accumulation dividend ETFs are two different ways in which ETFs pay out dividends to their investors.

Distribution ETFs pay out dividends regularly, usually quarterly or annually, in the form of cash payments to shareholders. This means that the dividends are paid out of the fund's current income and are taxed as ordinary income for the year they are received.

On the other hand, accumulation ETFs reinvest dividends into the fund rather than paying them out to shareholders. This means that the dividends are used to purchase additional shares of the ETF, effectively increasing the investor's holdings in the fund. This type of dividend reinvestment can compound over time, potentially leading to a more significant return for the investor in the long run. However, taxes on the dividends are deferred until the investor sells their shares, at which point they may be taxed as capital gains.

In summary, the main difference between distribution and accumulation dividend ETFs is how they pay out dividends to investors. Distribution ETFs pay out dividends in cash, while accumulation ETFs reinvest the dividends to purchase additional shares.

Beware of the Expense Ratio

The expense ratio is the fee associated with owning an ETF. It is a management charge paid to the fund company for investing in the fund. The expense ratio is a percentage of your total investment in the fund and represents the cost you'll incur annually. For example, if a fund has an expense ratio of 0.5%, you'll pay $50 per year for every $10,000 you invest in the fund.

It's important to note that the expense ratio is an annual cost. Still, it is typically taken out of the fund's net asset value daily for ETFs, making it virtually imperceptible to the investor. In addition, the cost is incurred regardless of how long you have owned the fund, so selling the fund just before the anniversary will not reduce the expense ratio.

However, in recent years, expense ratios have been declining as cheaper passive ETFs gain popularity.

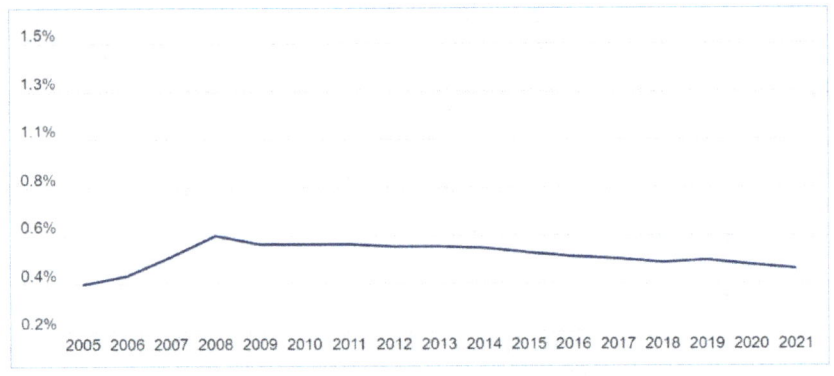

Figure 20 – ETF Expense Ratio over time. Source: www.bankrate.com

Dividend on SPY

The SPDR S&P 500 ETF distributes dividends to investors by collecting them in a non-interest-bearing account, then distributing them proportionally at the end of each fiscal quarter. Some other ETFs may instead reinvest dividends into the fund, which can affect the fund's performance depending on market conditions.

The Dividend Yield is as low as 1.65%, which could be more attractive. This is why we have the next section.

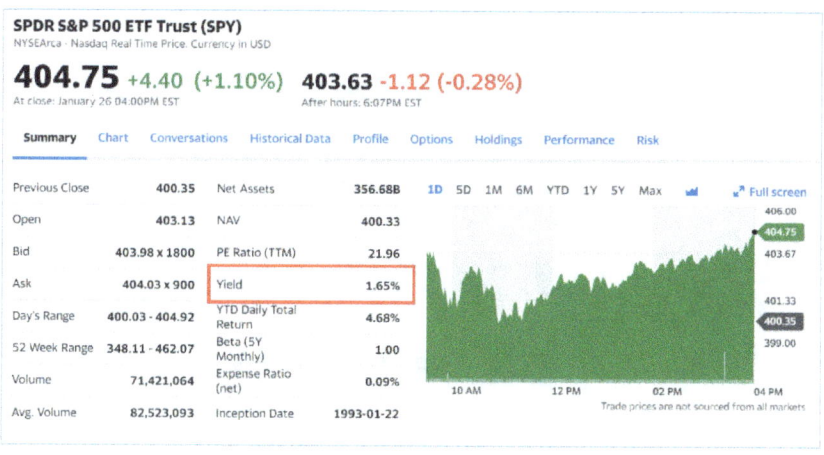

Figure 21 – Highlighted the Dividend Yield of SPY ETF as presented by Yahoo! Finance.

ETFs with High Dividend Yields

Here is my collection of 5 High Dividend Yield ETFs:

1. Fidelity International High Dividend ETF (FIDI) – **4.75%**
2. SPDR S&P Global Dividend (WDIV) – **4.83%**
3. iShares Core High Dividend ETF (HDV) – **3.54%**
4. Schwab Us Dividend Equity ETF (SCHD) – **3.35%**
5. iShares International Select Dividend ETF (IDV) – **6.76%**

Be aware that the higher the Dividend Yield, the higher the potential risk associated. Nothing comes for free.

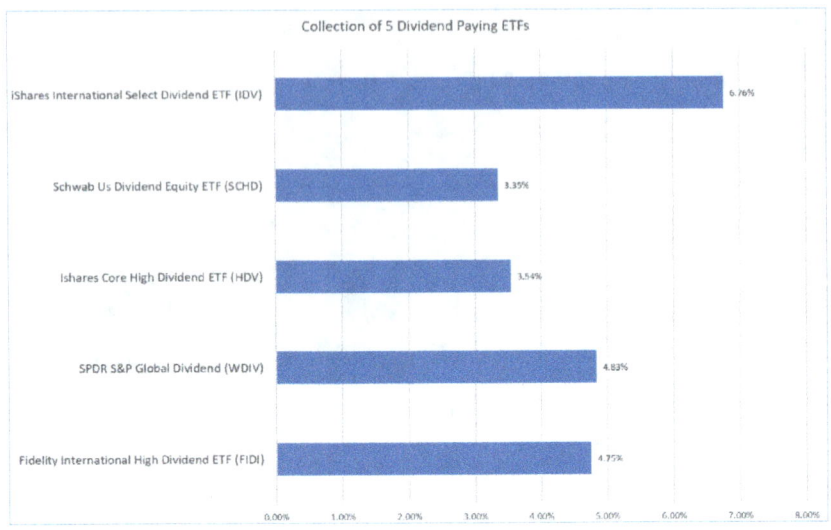

Figure 22 - My collection of 5 High Dividend Yield ETFs

I don't have anything more to say about it. If you have reached this point, you already have some good perspectives about the subject. I will compress most of the information into a short checklist in the next chapter.

6. Dividend Checklist

A dividend checklist can be helpful for investors because it helps them to evaluate and identify companies that are likely to provide stable and growing dividends with minimal effort.

We all know that you probably won't have the time to make an in-depth analysis. Here is how having some Check Points can help you as an easy first step for stock evaluation.

Here we go:

☐ **Consistency of dividends**

Look for stocks that have a history of consistently paying dividends. **Ten or more years is a good indication.**

☐ **Dividend yield**

Consider the current dividend yield, which is the annual dividend payment divided by the stock price. A higher yield may indicate a more attractive investment opportunity; however, it might be unsafe. **So run from stocks with a yield of over 10%.** I target an average portfolio yield of 5%.

☐ **Dividend growth rate**

Look for stocks that have a history of increasing their dividends over time. Again, **look for ten years or more.**

☐ **Payout ratio**

The payout ratio is the percentage of earnings a company pays out as dividends. A lower payout ratio may indicate that a company has more room to increase dividends in the future. **Under 75% is excellent.**

☐ **Financial Health**

Look for strong financial companies, including a healthy balance sheet and solid revenue and earnings growth. **Debt-to-Equity Ratio** is a good metric here. The lower it is, the better. **Look for values under 100%.**

☐ **Valuation**

Ensure the stock is reasonably priced in relation to its earnings and dividends. Use at least Price-to-Earnings Ratio to check the valuation. The lower it is, the better. It depends on the industry, but generally, a **P/E Ratio under 20 is considered good**, as it is not far from the market average.

☐ **Capital Appreciation and Total Return**

We are talking about dividends, but it would be good if the stock stays strong and you are not losing money. Look for a reasonable total return. **Let's say 100% in the last ten years.**

I prepared a list of a few dividend stocks that reflect the criteria mentioned in the checklist. Of course, only a few stocks will fulfill all the requirements. It is up to you what importance you give to each of them, but it is crucial to make acknowledged decisions.

Symbol ▲	Price	Yield FWD	Div Growth 5Y	Years of Growth	Payout Ratio	Debt to Equity	P/E FWD	10Y Total Return
ABBV	147.21	4.02%	16.92%	9 Years	41.78%	436.76%	10.69	488.74%
AMT	221.56	2.82%	17.47%	10 Years	93.64%	378.79%	34.63	235.51%
AVGO	595.62	3.07%	28.57%	11 Years	44.90%	176.04%	14.70	2,170.38%
CCI	146.72	4.23%	8.91%	8 Years	154.79%	375.35%	39.12	173.94%
DKL	50.81	8.08%	7.09%	8 Years	107.97%	NM	13.57	347.09%
EPD	26.51	7.45%	2.43%	23 Years	78.81%	107.70%	10.49	77.36%
IBM	135.06	4.91%	3.18%	23 Years	72.26%	245.28%	14.20	1.48%
IIPR	87.44	8.33%	66.79%	5 Years	130.77%	15.32%	16.21	-
IRM	54.93	4.61%	2.03%	0 Years	141.37%	2,068.98%	30.36	218.56%
MO	44.15	8.49%	7.70%	53 Years	76.83%	NM	9.20	133.67%
MPW	12.96	9.22%	3.86%	10 Years	55.29%	107.28%	6.36	80.87%
NEE	76.14	2.23%	11.59%	27 Years	-	131.41%	24.56	448.19%
NEM	53.58	4.06%	54.49%	0 Years	100.00%	28.63%	28.71	54.53%
O	68.52	4.39%	3.86%	26 Years	273.43%	62.88%	31.21	152.77%
OHI	29.04	9.35%	1.08%	0 Years	154.02%	135.67%	-	129.09%
STAG	35.87	4.14%	0.77%	11 Years	109.59%	71.35%	-	207.06%
T	19.95	5.55%	-5.69%	0 Years	-	145.30%	8.05	39.08%
TROW	117.26	4.19%	16.05%	36 Years	49.58%	4.28%	15.92	117.49%

Figure 23 – Example of key metrics for a collection of dividend stocks

57

7. Portfolio of Dividend Stocks

The definition of the portfolio is simple: it is a collection of securities held by an investor, such as stocks, bonds, and commodities.

Different portfolio construction techniques refer to the methods used to optimize the composition and diversification of a portfolio to achieve specific investment objectives.

These techniques involve using quantitative analysis and mathematical portfolio modeling to identify and select the most appropriate assets for inclusion in the portfolio.

There are several advantages of using such techniques, including:

Improved Tradeoff Between Risk and Return

- Portfolio Construction Techniques use mathematical models to optimize the risk & return, enabling investors to achieve the desired gains based on their targets.

Diversification and Asset Allocation

- Techniques use various sophisticated methods to help identify less correlated assets, helping reduce the risk in Investors' Portfolios and improving overall diversification.

Transparency and Expectancy

- Portfolio construction techniques offer better transparency and control for investors by providing detailed and actionable information on the portfolio's composition and performance. This allows investors to clearly understand their investments, their characteristics, and how they contribute to the overall portfolio performance.

We will not explain the different techniques and the theory behind them here. Instead, what we will do is build 3 dividend portfolios that have three different targets. We will use the stocks presented in Figure 23 as a basis and build the portfolios by selecting the best possible combination to meet each target.

Before we get started, please note that any of this portfolio back-testing does not guarantee future behavior.

Minimum Volatility Dividend Portfolio

A minimum volatility portfolio is a portfolio that aims to minimize the volatility (or risk) of the returns while still generating a positive return. The goal is to provide a more stable return over time rather than a portfolio that experiences large swings in value due to market fluctuations. Minimum volatility portfolios are often used by risk-averse investors who prioritize capital preservation over high returns.

As controversial as it might sound, this can be better achieved not by holding low-volatility assets but rather by holding assets that are not correlated to each other.

Mathematical Modeling and Modern Portfolio Theory are outside the scope of this book. However, the logic behind this is simple: when one stock goes down, the second goes up, the third stays stable, and so on. Indeed, this is the same logic as the one advising to invest in different industries, as different industries perform differently throughout an economic cycle.

Luckily for all of us, free tools can assist investors in building and optimizing their portfolios. I use PortfolioVisualizer.

That being said, let's analyze the performance of the following portfolio:

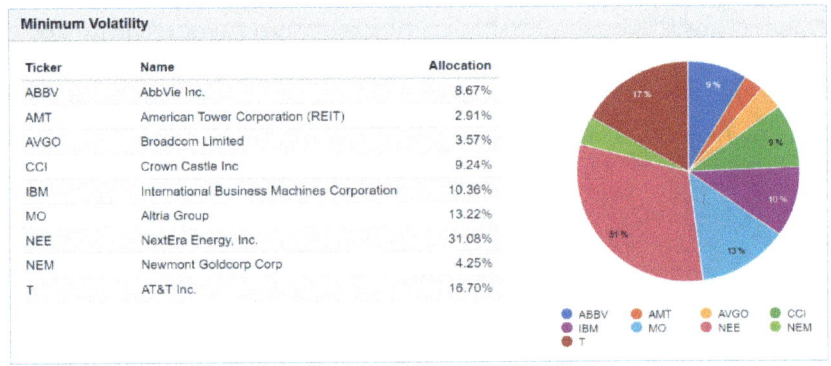

Minimum Volatility

Ticker	Name	Allocation
ABBV	AbbVie Inc.	8.67%
AMT	American Tower Corporation (REIT)	2.91%
AVGO	Broadcom Limited	3.57%
CCI	Crown Castle Inc	9.24%
IBM	International Business Machines Corporation	10.36%
MO	Altria Group	13.22%
NEE	NextEra Energy, Inc.	31.08%
NEM	Newmont Goldcorp Corp	4.25%
T	AT&T Inc.	16.70%

Figure 24 – Selection and Allocation of stocks for Minimum Volatility target

To get a better feeling about the achievement, we will compare this "Minimum Volatility" Portfolio with a portfolio composed of the same stocks but equally weighted and a simple 100% S&P500 portfolio.

Performance Summary

Portfolio	Initial Balance	Final Balance	CAGR	Stdev	Best Year	Worst Year	Max. Drawdown	Sharpe Ratio
Equal Distribution	$10,000	$53,663	18.30%	15.13%	38.72%	-9.66%	-23.33%	1.14
Minimum Volatility	$10,000	$44,353	16.06%	13.16%	30.91%	-6.84%	-17.37%	1.15
S&P500 Only	$10,000	$32,358	12.46%	14.76%	32.31%	-18.17%	-23.93%	0.82

Figure 25 – Comparison between Equal Distribution, Minimum Volatility, and S&P500 Only Portfolios

Please note that all the dividends were re-invested in each case, and no portfolio re-balancing was done. Also, the analysis is constrained between January 2013 and December 2022 due to the availability of ABBV.

OK, so what can we see here?

As expected, our "Minimum Volatility" Portfolio does not have the best performance, but this was not the target.

However, it still significantly outperformed the "S&P500 Only" Portfolio, with a Final Balance of over $44,000. And what is even more important, this was achieved while keeping volatility (StDev = Standard Deviation) of only 13.16%, the lowest among the three.

Target achieved!

If this does not mean anything, look at the Worst Year and the Maximum Drawdown. Both of them look significantly better compared to the other two portfolios.

This means we did not only "beat the market" we did it by also having a more stable growth compared to the market.

Figure 26 – Performance of Equal Distribution, Minimum Volatility, and S&P500 Only Portfolios over time

By the way, the portfolio's volatility is significantly lower than any stock in its composition. This is what I promised right from the beginning.

Performance Summary

Portfolio		Final Balance	CAGR	Stdev	Best Year	Worst Year	Max. Drawdown	Sharpe Ratio
Minimum Volatility		$44,353	18.08%	13.16%	30.91%	-8.84%	-17.37% ❶	1.15

Portfolio Assets

Ticker	Name	Asset Contribution	CAGR	Stdev	Best Year	Worst Year	Max Drawdown	Sharpe Ratio
ABBV	AbbVie Inc.	$5,170	21.44%	25.82%	60.13%	-6.46%	-39.03%	0.85
AMT	American Tower Corporation (REIT)	$677	12.77%	19.62%	47.85%	-25.63%	-27.80%	0.87
AVGO	Broadcom Limited	$7,811	36.76%	28.66%	90.19%	-13.27%	-31.70%	1.22
CCI	Crown Castle Inc	$1,458	9.03%	18.91%	35.48%	-32.51%	-34.44%	0.56
IBM	International Business Machines Corporation	$143	1.30%	22.43%	25.19%	-22.56%	-37.18%	0.14
MO	Altria Group	$2,073	9.80%	22.30%	34.52%	-27.09%	-49.81%	0.50
NEE	NextEra Energy, Inc.	$16,414	20.17%	18.41%	42.69%	-8.58%	-23.52%	1.06
NEM	Newmont Goldcorp Corp	$110	2.33%	37.36%	90.11%	-48.51%	-63.39%	0.22
T	AT&T Inc	$486	2.60%	18.28%	45.62%	-22.24%	-37.45%	0.19

Figure 27 – Highlighted Standard Deviation of each stock and the whole portfolio.

But what if you are not a risk-averse investor and would like to achieve better returns while allowing a moderate risk increase?

Then you have to move to the following portfolio with a higher-risk budget.

Maximum Sharpe Ratio Dividend Portfolio

The Sharpe ratio is a way to measure the performance of an investment by adjusting for the amount of risk taken. It is calculated by subtracting the risk-free rate (like a Treasury bond) from the return of an investment and then dividing that by the volatility of the return.

The higher the Sharpe ratio, the better the investment's performance was given the level of risk. It is used to compare the performance of different assets, with a higher ratio indicating better performance. It's a way to find out how much return you are getting for every unit of risk you take.

Let's build the following portfolio starting from the initial list from Figure 23.

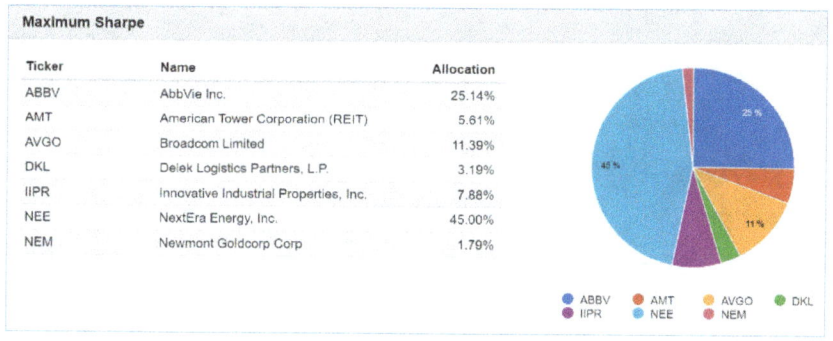

Figure 28 – Maximum Sharpe Ratio Portfolio

Again, we will compare this portfolio with an equally weighted alternative and the simple S&P500.

Portfolio	Initial Balance	Final Balance	CAGR	Stdev	Best Year	Worst Year	Max. Drawdown	Sharpe Ratio
Equal Distribution	$10,000	$34,786	22.74%	22.24%	58.16%	-29.23%	-38.34%	0.98
Maximum Sharpe	$10,000	$38,991	23.43%	18.53%	46.70%	-17.98%	-27.45%	1.17
S&P500 Only	$10,000	$19,393	11.50%	16.97%	31.22%	-18.17%	-23.93%	0.66

Figure 29 - Comparison between Equal Distribution, Maximum Sharpe, and S&P500 Only Portfolios

This time we got even more impressive results, as the "Maximum Sharpe" Portfolio achieved the highest return and Sharpe Ratio! This is also illustrated in the last column, where it has the highest value, as you can see.

Please note that this time the analysis was limited to the period from December 2016 to December 2022 due to the availability of IIPR.

The performance can also be easily observed on the following chart:

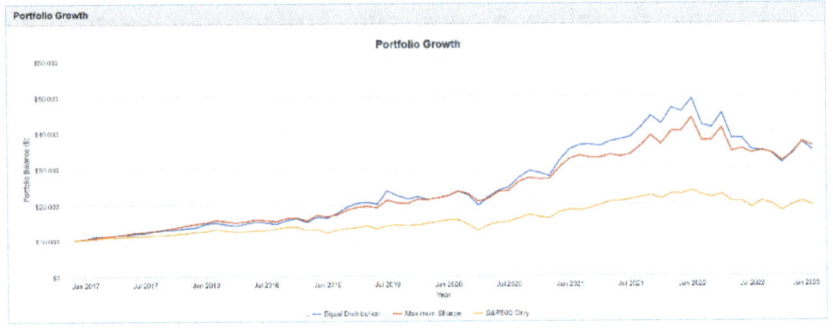

Figure 30 - Performance of Equal Distribution, Maximum Sharpe, and S&P500 Only Portfolios over time

As we did in the previous example, let's prove that the Sharpe Ratio of the presented portfolio is better than any of the individual stocks.

Performance Summary

Portfolio	Final Balance	CAGR	Stdev	Best Year	Worst Year	Max. Drawdown	Sharpe Ratio
Maximum Sharpe	$35,991	23.43%	18.53%	48.70%	-17.98%	-27.45%	1.17

Portfolio Assets

Ticker	Name	Asset Contribution	CAGR	Stdev	Best Year	Worst Year	Max Drawdown	Sharpe Ratio
ABBV	AbbVie Inc.	$6,219	22.71%	27.53%	60.13%	-0.98%	-36.03%	0.84
AMT	American Tower Corporation (REIT)	$782	15.14%	20.70%	47.85%	-25.83%	-27.80%	0.73
AVGO	Broadcom Limited	$3,426	25.63%	27.89%	56.43%	-13.27%	-31.70%	0.93
DKL	Delek Logistics Partners, L.P.	$707	21.18%	62.54%	48.26%	2.06%	-70.56%	0.56
IIPR	Innovative Industrial Properties, Inc.	$4,117	35.06%	90.81%	161.25%	-58.39%	-64.81%	0.75
NEE	NextEra Energy, Inc.	$10,834	22.06%	19.50%	42.89%	-6.58%	-23.52%	1.07
NEM	Newmont Goldcorp Corp	$128	9.18%	30.07%	40.26%	-20.80%	-47.52%	0.40

Figure 31 - Highlighted the Sharpe Ratio of each stock and the whole portfolio.

Again, the target was achieved!

So far, so good, but what does everything of this have to do with dividends? To answer this question, let's build a new portfolio targeting the top yields.

Maximum Yield Portfolio

This time we will make our analysis slightly different. We will not compare any longer with an S&P500 portfolio. Instead, we will pick the top 7 stocks with the highest dividend yields from Figure 23 and compare their Equally Weighted and the Maximum Sharpe variations with the overall Maximum Sharpe portfolio presented in Figure 28.

So, here it goes:

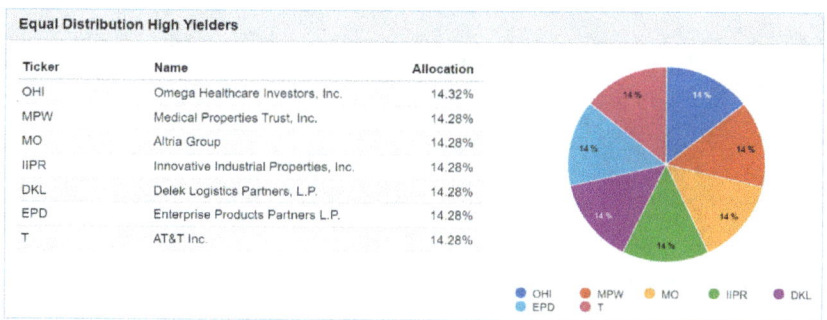

Figure 32 – Equal Distribution Portfolio of Top 7 Yielders from Figure 23

In the attempt to make an optimization step and maximize the Sharpe Ratio of the High Yielders portfolio, we barely end up having only three stocks:

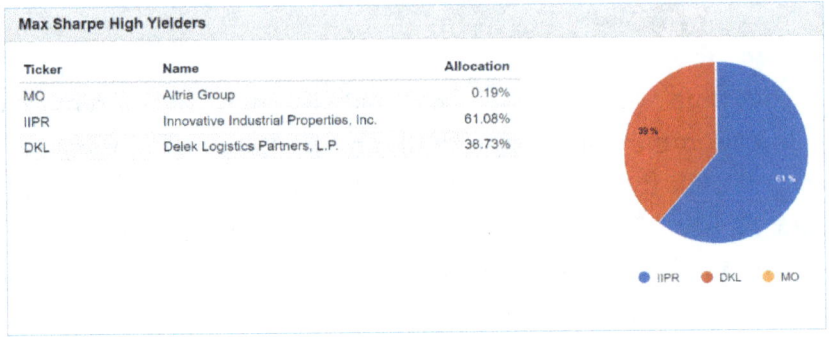

Max Sharpe High Yielders		
Ticker	Name	Allocation
MO	Altria Group	0.19%
IIPR	Innovative Industrial Properties, Inc.	61.08%
DKL	Delek Logistics Partners, L.P.	38.73%

Figure 33 – Re-selection among the top 7 yielders from Figure 32 to get the maximum Sharpe Ratio Portfolio

Now, let's compare all three:

Performance Summary							
Portfolio	Initial Balance	Final Balance	CAGR	Stdev	Best Year	Worst Year	Max. Drawdown
Equal Distribution High Yielders	$10,000	$22,569	14.32%	27.32%	44.24%	-37.59%	-40.73%
Max Sharpe High Yielders	$10,000	$50,501	30.50%	46.36%	123.00%	-51.26%	-55.71%
Max Sharpe Overall	$10,000	$35,991	23.43%	18.53%	46.70%	-17.96%	-27.45%

Figure 34 – Comparison of Equal Distribution High Yielders, Max Sharpe High Yielders, and Max Sharpe Overall

It is not easy to digest, and the conclusion is at least controversial. Let's eat it in two bites.

First, the performance of the Max Sharpe optimization of the High Yielders is simply unbelievable. It beats, by far, the other two portfolios. However, look at the Volatility (StDev) and the Maximum Drawdown. Would you be able to sleep well at night? I doubt. Remember you hold only two stocks mainly.

Second, we can easily observe a significant outperformance of the Max Sharpe Overall, compared to the Equal Distribution of the High Yielders. Furthermore, this was achieved by significantly better volatility and drawdowns.

Which of the three would you like to have? For myself, I have a clear answer.

Conclusion

You might ask what the key message of this chapter is. First, don't blindly focus on the highest-yield companies and throw your money into them. Instead, always try to see the big picture and analyze all the potential investments from a complete portfolio perspective.

A further essential note is that in all three cases, there was no portfolio rebalancing at all. Of course, if we did an annual re-balancing, the figures would look different, but the main conclusion would remain the same.

I leave this task to you. Feel free to experiment with PortfolioVisualizer and assess the impact of any stock addition on the overall portfolio performance and behavior.

Final words

Of course, you can look at paid subscriptions and many other ratios to compare companies and decide which one you like, but what I wrote here in this book is the best of my experience, studies, and experiments. I use these methods every day and whenever I invest in the market.

Thank you very much for staying with me until this book's end.

Invest wisely and have a great investment adventure!

Alexandru Artenie

Founder of ARTInvest

Iasi, 2023

https://www.art-invest.net/

Annex - List of Mentioned Tools

FastGraphs

DividendRadar

SeekingAlpha

Yahoo! Finance

PortfolioVisualizer

Google Finance

TIPRANKS Dividend Calculator

List of Figures

For Notes